AVATAR

COLORING BOOK

Project Art Editor Stefan Georgiou
Production Editor Siu Yin Chan
Senior Production Controller Mary Slater
Managing Editor Emma Grange
Managing Art Editor Vicky Short
Publishing Director Mark Searle

Illustrated by Maurizio Campidelli

DK would like to thank: James Cameron, Jon Landau,
Joshua Izzo and Reymundo Perez at Lightstorm,
Nicole Spiegel at Disney, and Maurizio Campidelli.

First American Edition, 2023
Published in the United States by DK Publishing
1745 Broadway, 20th Floor, New York, NY 10019

A catalog record for this book is available from the Library of Congress
ISBN: 978-0-7440-9762-7

DK books are available at special discounts when purchased in bulk
for sales promotions, premiums, fund-raising, or educational use.
For details, contact: DK Publishing Special Markets,
1745 Broadway, 20th Floor, New York, NY 10019
SpecialSales@dk.com

Printed and bound in China

www.dk.com

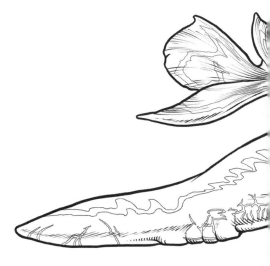

COLORING BOOK

ILLUSTRATED BY
MAURIZIO CAMPIDELLI

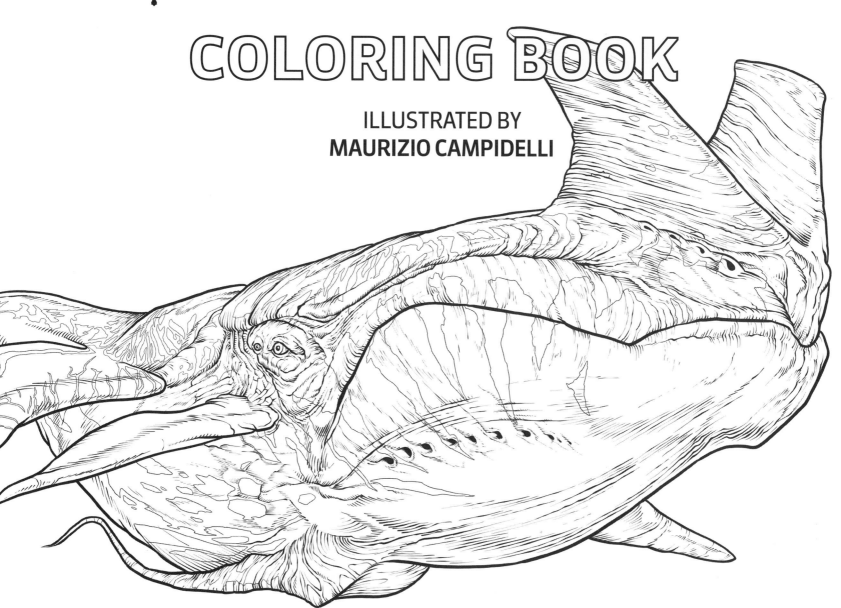

HAMMERHEAD
TITANOTHERE

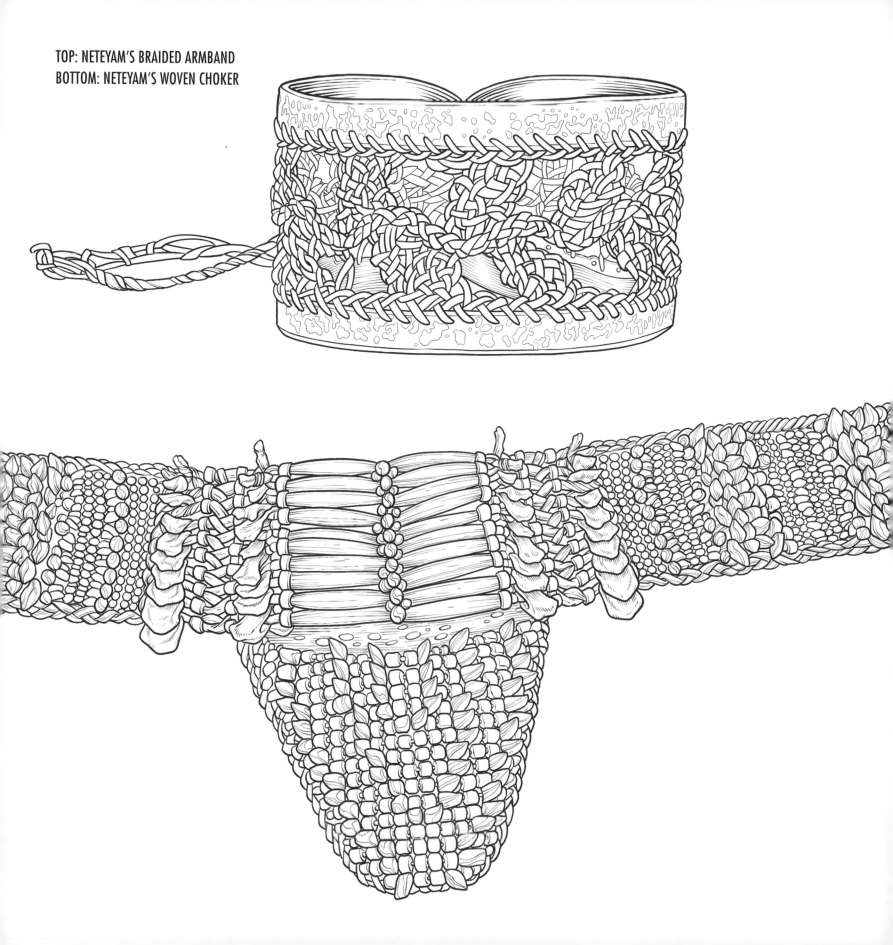

TOP: NETEYAM'S BRAIDED ARMBAND
BOTTOM: NETEYAM'S WOVEN CHOKER

NETEYAM

NEYTIRI'S BONE COLLAR

LO'AK'S ARMGUARD

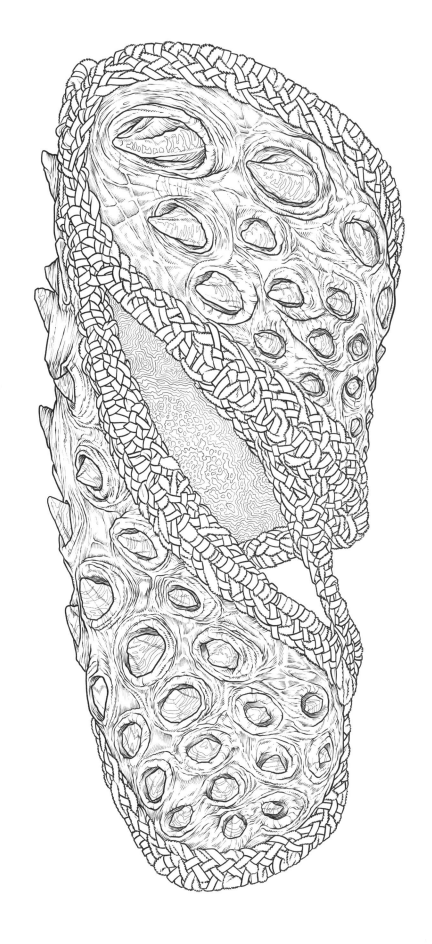

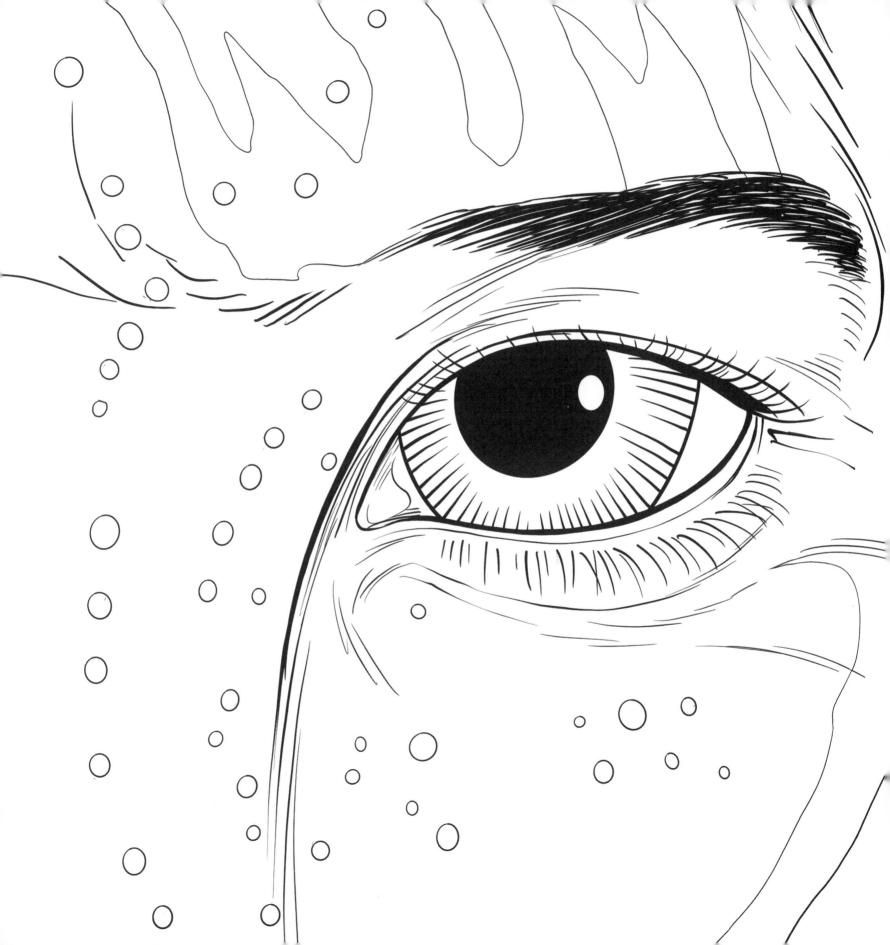

MO'AT

EYTUKAN

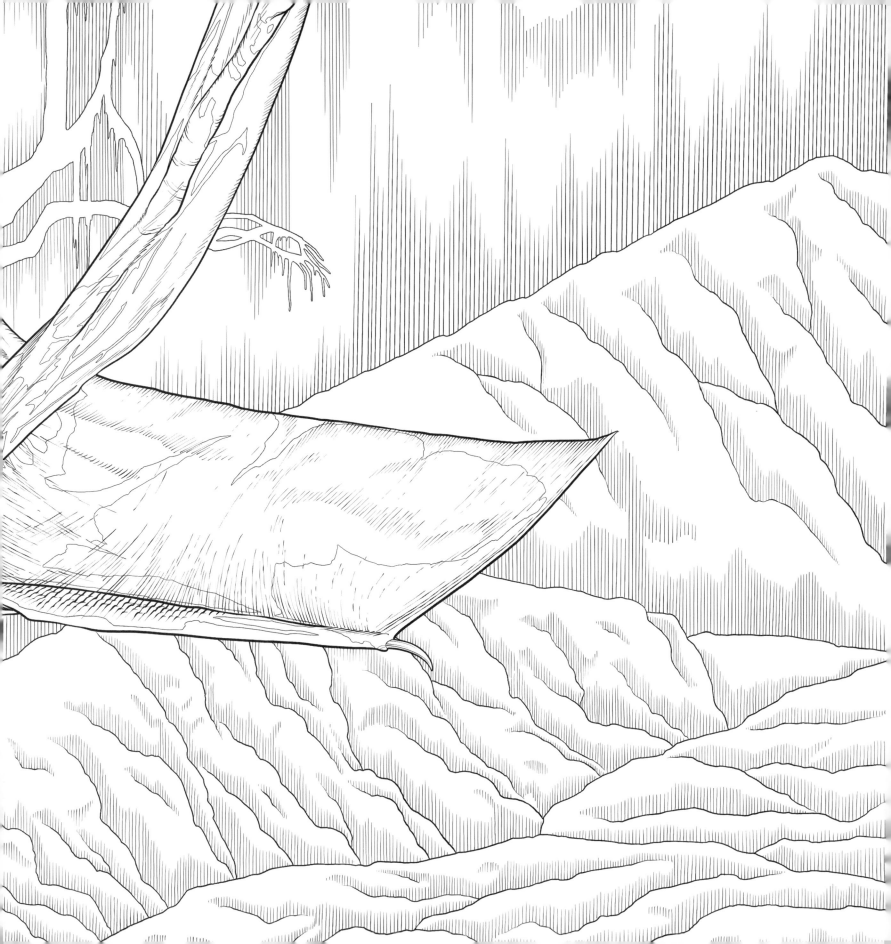

GOBLIN THISTLE

DAKTERON FLOWER

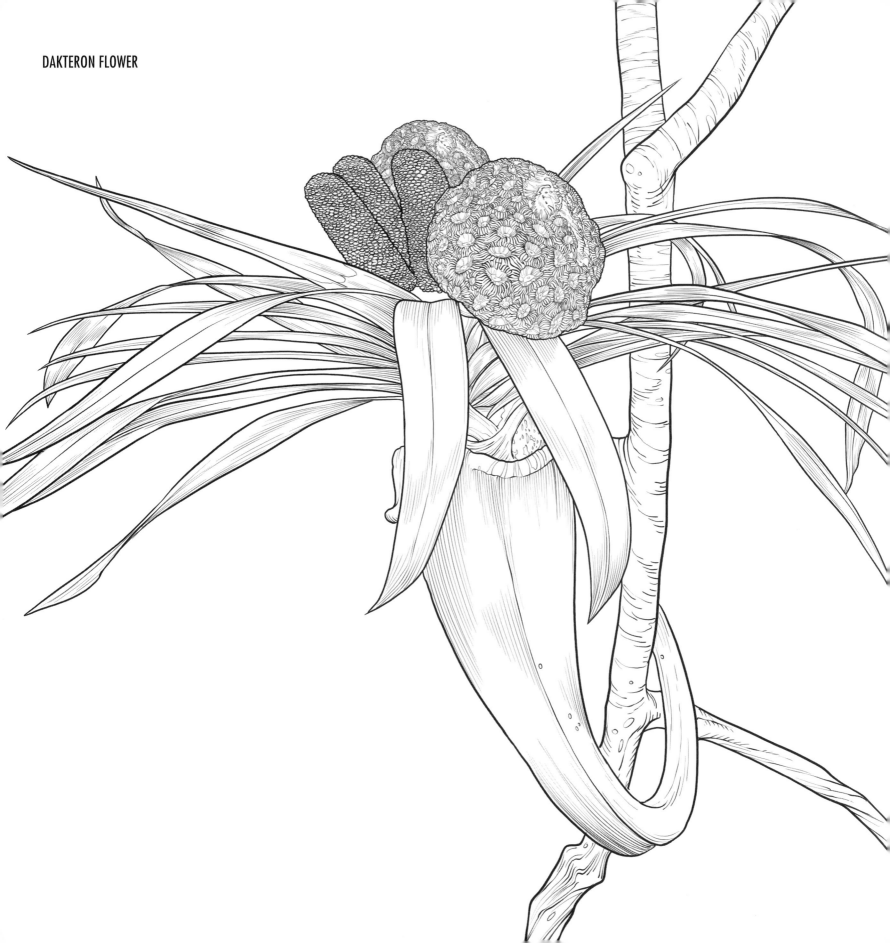

TOP: HUNTING KNIFE
BOTTOM: KNIFE SHEATH

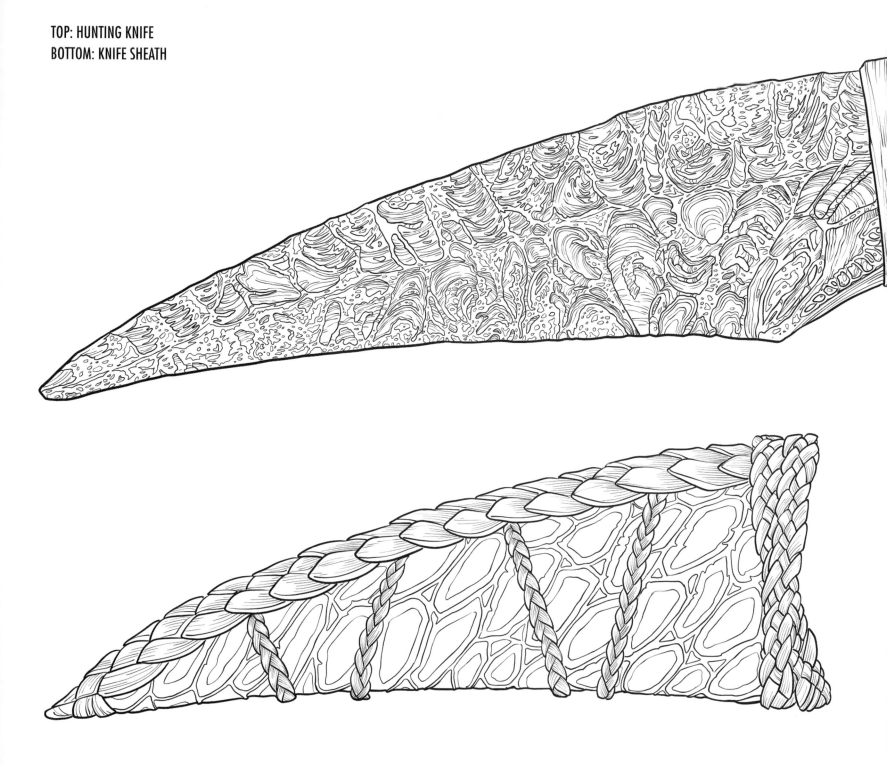

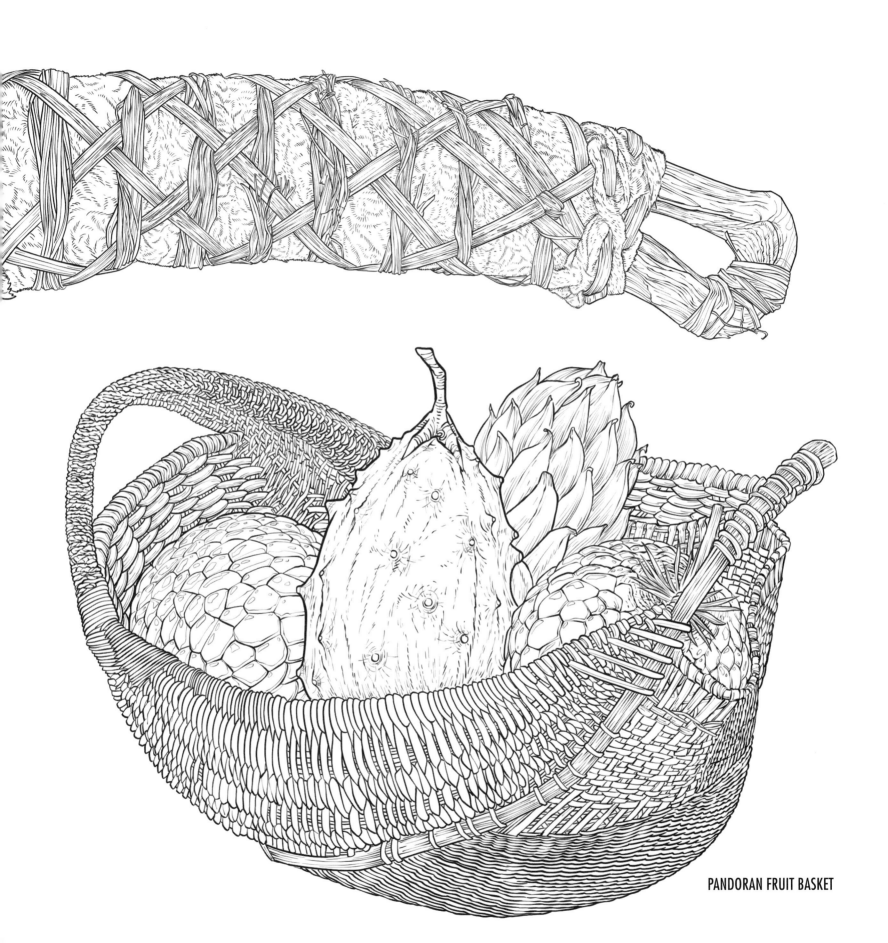

PANDORAN FRUIT BASKET

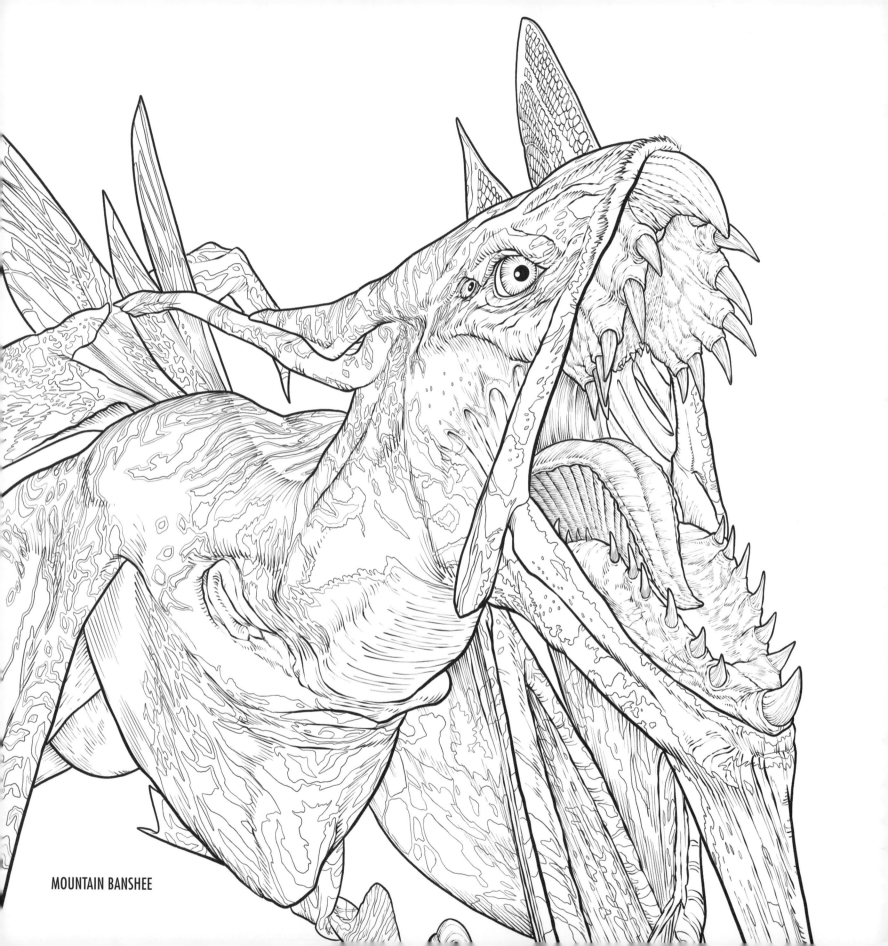

MOUNTAIN BANSHEE

RONAL

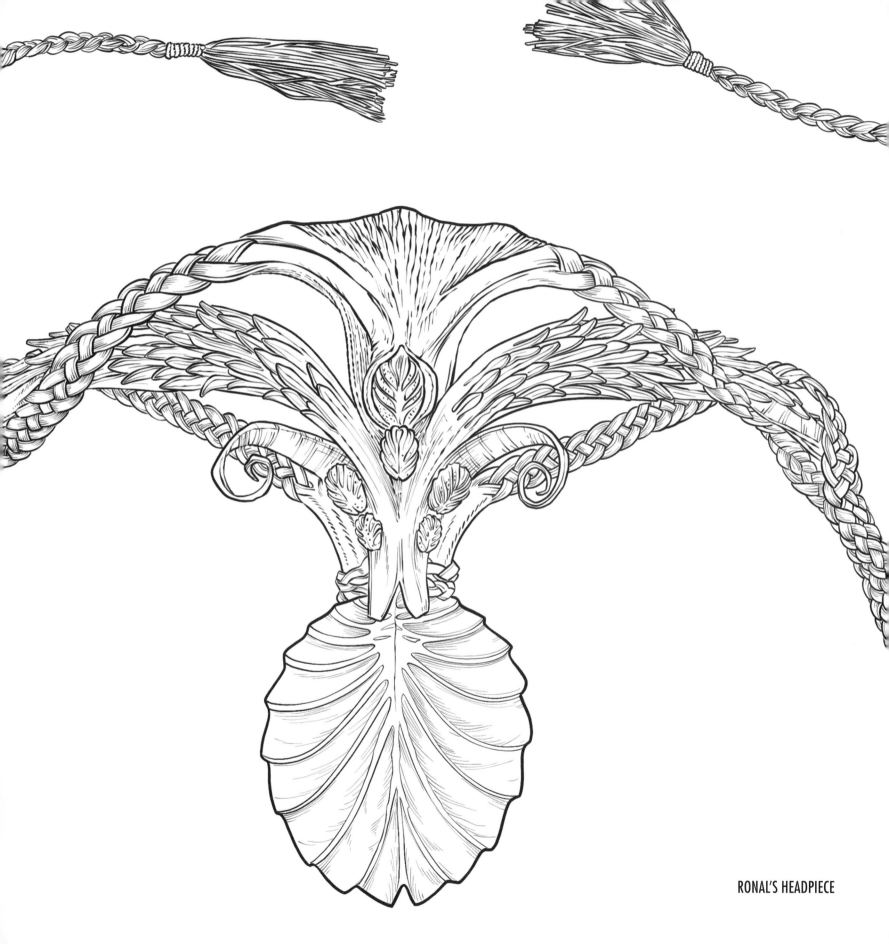

RONAL'S HEADPIECE

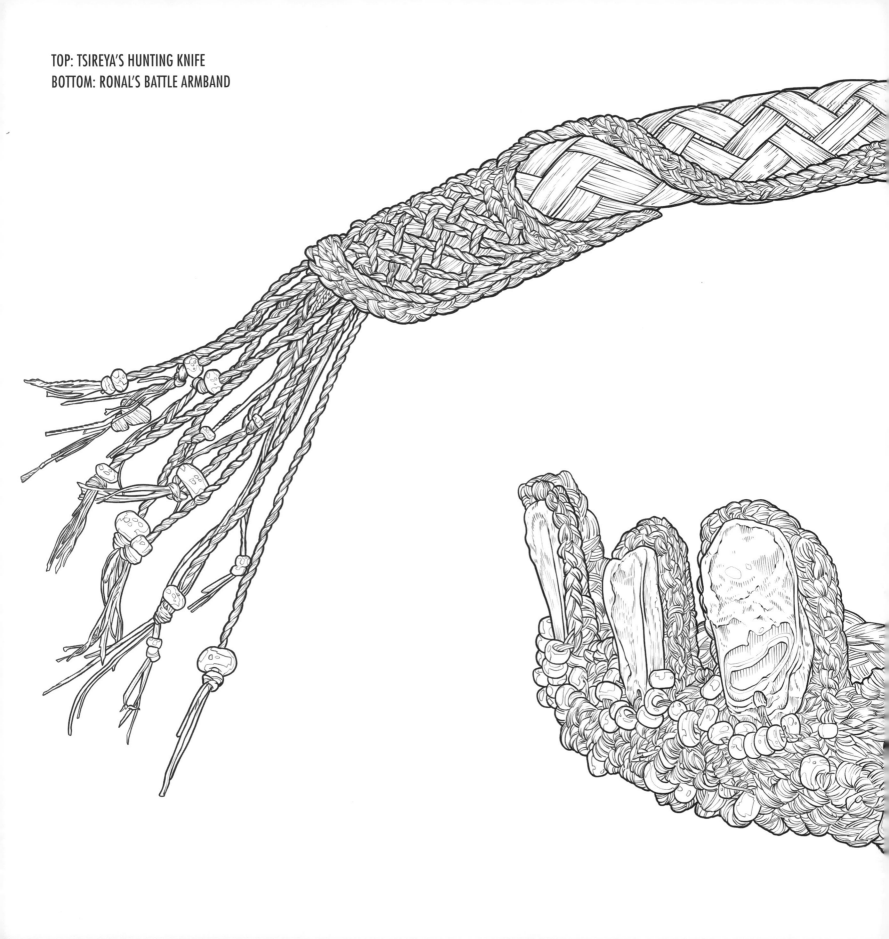

TOP: TSIREYA'S HUNTING KNIFE
BOTTOM: RONAL'S BATTLE ARMBAND

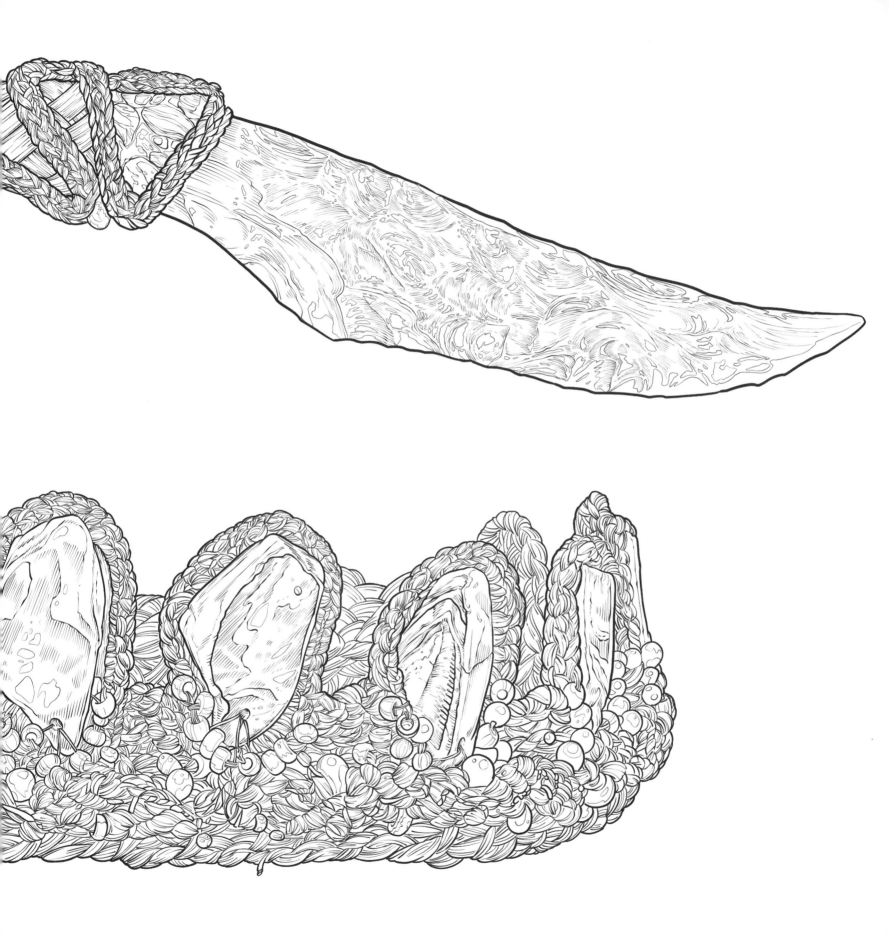

TULKUN

GREAT LEONOPTERYX

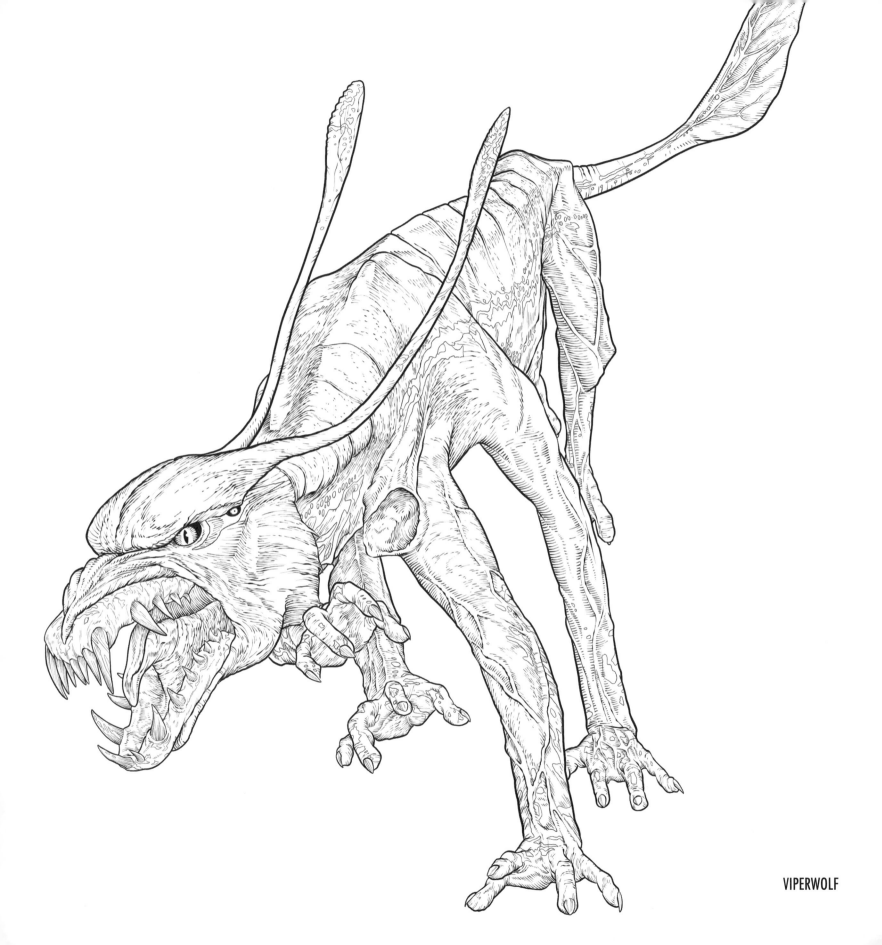

VIPERWOLF

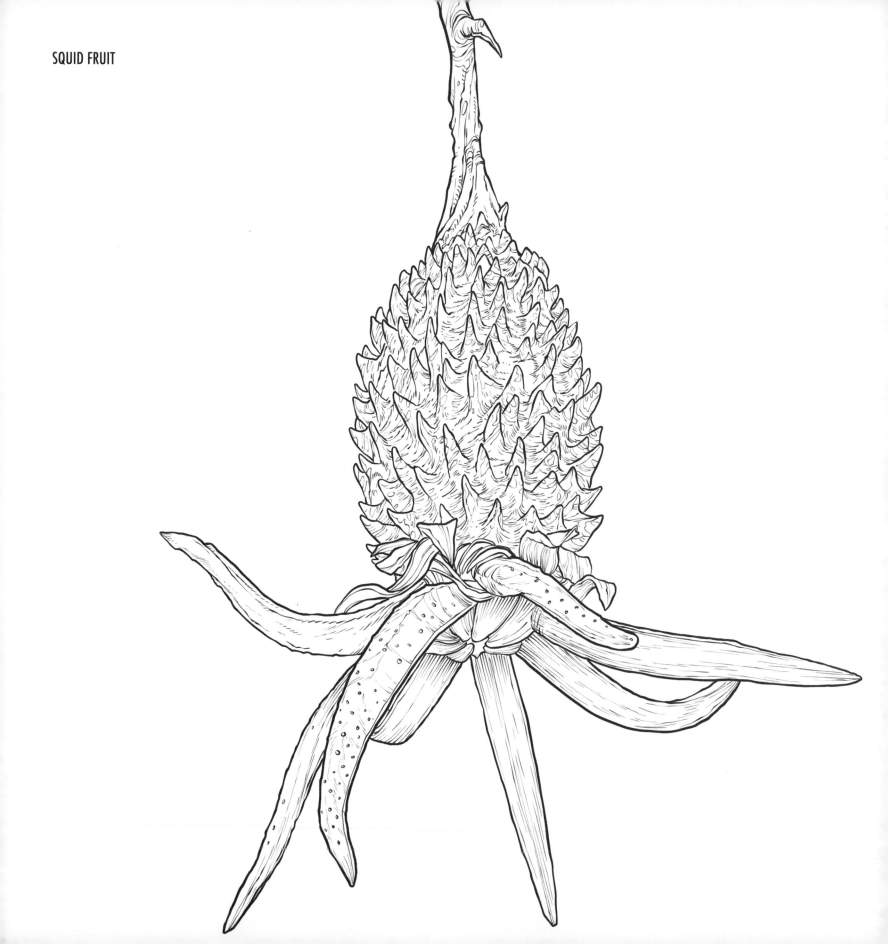

ILU

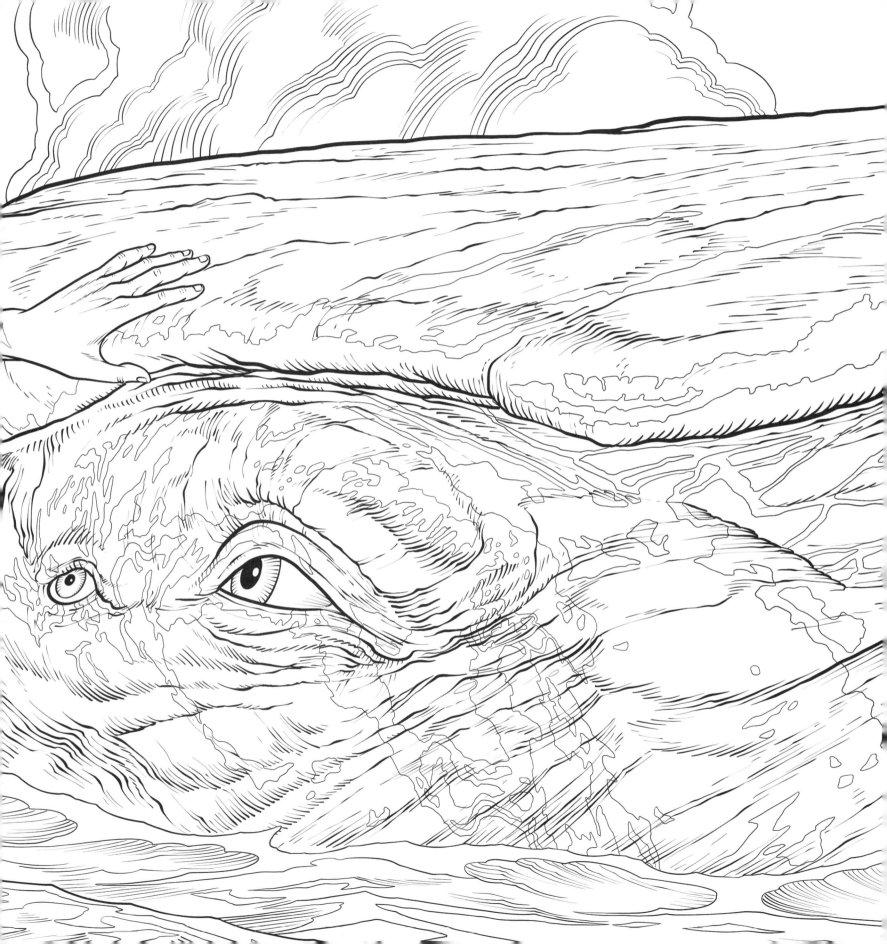

CELIA FRUIT